SPECIALS!

THE MAKING OF THE UK: 1500 TO 1750

Elisabeth Karalis Isaac
Robert Isaac

Folens Publishers

INTRODUCTION

SPECIALS! are designed to open up vital areas of the National Curriculum to secondary school children with learning difficulties. The use of minimal text, lively, relevant activities and the opportunity of presenting work orally and visually, will spark enthusiasm in even the most reluctant learners and give them a much-needed feeling of success in their work.

The Making of the UK: 1500 to 1750 provides a programme of work for children at Key Stage 3. It concentrates on two main themes: the political unification of Britain and the changing relationship between the monarch, Parliament and the people.

The activities are designed to develop pupils' knowledge and understanding of history - Attainment Target 1. A matrix is included on page 6 in order that teachers may identify which strands of the Attainment Target are being covered by each unit.

At the end of the book there are two simple record sheets, one for the pupil and one for the teacher. Once completed, these can be the focus of teacher/pupil consultation.

Illustrations by Eric Jones

Cover by Abacus Art

First published 1993 by Folens Limited, Albert House, Apex Business Centre, Boscombe Road, Dunstable, LU5 4RL, England.

ISBN 185276293-4

Printed by Ashford Colour Press.

CONTENTS

TEACHERS' NOTES

National Curriculum History focuses on the development of pupils' knowledge and understanding of history. These resource sheets will give all pupils access to the demands of the Programme of Study and encourage historical understanding.

Title	Purpose
Did You Know?	To gain or confirm a basic knowledge of the UK and Parliament.
A United Kingdom?	To learn that union was an assertion of English power and to understand that there had been much conflict within the regions which made up the UK.
Tudor and Stuart Monarchs	To consolidate knowledge of the chronological sequence of Tudor and Stuart monarchs.
Power and Parliament 1500	To gain an understanding of social ranking in England and access to power.
The Common People	To introduce the idea of the common people (as distinct from the Commoners in Parliament) and to consider their quality of life.
Henry Rules/King, Pope and Parliament	To develop an understanding of the issues of power and religion underlying the break with Rome. To emphasise the power of the Tudor monarchy and Henry's willingness to call upon Parliament for assistance.
Protestants and Power	To revise the significant events in the development of England's becoming a Protestant country. To understand how loyalty to England and Protestantism became intertwined.
The Civil Wars	To gain or confirm knowledge of the Parliamentary and Royalist areas of support in England.
Money Matters	To gain an understanding of the importance of taxation in the deterioration of relations between the King and Parliament.
Religion	To increase understanding of religious divisions, and to explore the different attitudes towards Charles' and Laud's religious changes.
Monarch and Parliament 1625-1629	To understand early developments in the conflict between the King and Parliament and how they reflected the King's personality and ideas held by those opposing him in Parliament.
Dismissing Parliament	To analyse two sources that show the increasing difficulties facing the King because of Buckingham's unpopularity and his own actions against Parliament.
Personal Rule 1629-1640	To understand later developments in the conflict between the King and Parliament and how they reflected the King's ideas and character.
Monarch and Parliament 1640-1641	To consolidate understanding of the changes in the balance of power between Parliament and monarch.
For or Against Parliament?	To consider the attitudes of different people to Parliament, the King, and events in England.
For or Against the King?	To look at the quickening pace of events in 1641-2, and understand the lead up to war.
Civil War Battles	To study the locations of the main battles and to consider the consequences of major events in the war.

Title	Purpose
The Soldiers	To learn about the appearance of Cavaliers and Roundheads, before and after 1644.
News and Headlines	To gain additional knowledge about events and to distinguish between fact and opinion.
Women and the War	To appreciate that women took an active role in the war.
End of War?	To gain an understanding of the complexities of 1646 and to consider the King's response to the situation.
Death of the King	To learn that regicide was not supported by most Members of Parliament, and that the death of the King was organised by a determined minority.
The Rise of Cromwell	To increase understanding of the role of Cromwell and the army between 1646 and 1655.
Opinion Poll	To apply pupils' understanding of Royalist and Parliamentarian attitudes.
The Speaker and Parliament	To learn about significant events in the struggle between the King and Parliament, and to deepen understanding of the changing relationship between the two.
Restoration	To realise that events have a differing significance for people, according to their circumstances.
The Wheel of History	To consolidate knowledge of political events between 1640 and 1690.
Follow the Crown	To trace the succession through the Stuart line to the Hanoverians.
Joint Monarchs	To gain knowledge of the limitations placed upon the monarchy by the Bill of Rights. To compare the new balance of power between monarch and Parliament with the old balance of power.
Road Signs	To appreciate significant events in the development towards constitutional monarchy in the seventeenth century.
Plots and Prayers	To gain knowledge of the connections between power, politics and religion. To consider the effects of famous plots on popular opinion.
Religion, Politics and Science	To learn about the new political, religious and scientific ideas, and their effect on people's lives.
Science	To gain knowledge about the great developments in scientific thought during the seventeenth century, while appreciating the continuity of some beliefs and practices.
Uniting the Kingdom	To look at the main stages in the development of the United Kingdom.
Ireland	To understand the relations between England and Ireland: the increase of English power and the decline of Catholic land ownership.
Stuart to Hanover	To contrast the power of Hanoverian monarchs with the power enjoyed by the Tudors.
Parliament and Prime Ministers	To understand that government required Parliament's consent and to judge the extent to which 18th-century England was democratic.
Classes	To appreciate the enormous differences in wealth and lifestyle of the English social classes.
The Race	To revise knowledge of significant individuals in the development of constitutional monarchy.

"What is good practice in relation to special educational needs is good practice for all."

A Curriculum For All, National Curriculum Council, 1989.

THE NATIONAL CURRICULUM

The matrix below shows how each resource sheet meets the requirements of the Programme of Study and, where applicable, the strand within Attainment Target 1 as described in the Non-Statutory Guidance.

Page	Programme of Study	Attainment Target Strand
7	Crown and Parliament	Change and continuity
8	Political unification	Change and continuity
9	Monarchs - chronology	Not applicable
10	Crown and Parliament	Not applicable
11	Social classes	Change and continuity
12	Religious differences	Key features of past situations
13	Religious differences	Not applicable
14	Power of the monarchy	Causes and consequences
15	Civil War	Not applicable
16	Crown and Parliament	Causes and consequences
17	Religious differences	Key features of past situations
18	Crown and Parliament	Causes and consequences
19	Crown and Parliament	Key features of past situations
20	Crown and Parliament	Key features of past situations
21	Crown and Parliament	Change and continuity
22	Social classes	Key features of past situations
23	Crown and Parliament	Causes and consequences
24	Civil War	Causes and consequences
25	Civil War	Not applicable
26	Civil War	Key features of past situations
27	Civil War	Key features of past situations
28	Crown and Parliament	Key features of past situations
29	Crown and Parliament	Not applicable
30	Interregnum	Change and continuity
31	Crown and Parliament	Key features of past situations
32	Crown and Parliament	Change and continuity
33	Crown, Parliament and people/social classes	Key features of past situations
34	Crown and Parliament	Change and continuity
35	The Crown	Change and continuity
36	Crown, Parliament and people	Change and continuity
37	Crown, Parliament and people	Change and continuity
38	Roman Catholics and Anglicans	Key features of past situations
39	Changes in ideas	Change and continuity
40	Scientific changes	Change and continuity
41	Political unification	Change and continuity
42	England and Ireland	Causes and consequences
43	Crown and Parliament	Change and continuity
44	Crown, Parliament and people	Change and continuity
45	Social classes	Not applicable
46	Crown, Parliament and people	Change and continuity

DID YOU KNOW?

These islands are the British Isles. The United Kingdom (UK) is in the British Isles. Shade the United Kingdom and mark on the map: London, Edinburgh, Cardiff, Belfast.

REMEMBER

● A monarch of the UK is Head of the State. The monarch can be a king or queen. The present monarch is

● A Prime Minister is the leader of the Government in the UK. A Prime Minister can be a man or a woman. The present Prime Minister is

● The United Kingdom's Parliament meets in the House of Commons in London. There are 651 Members of Parliament (MPs). Citizens of the UK who are over eighteen vote for new MPs every four or five years. The party with more MPs than all the other parties put together becomes the Government. The present party with most MPs is

KEY

☐ - UNITED KINGDOM
L - LONDON   E - EDINBURGH
C - CARDIFF   B - BELFAST

SCOTLAND

NORTHERN IRELAND

EIRE

IRISH SEA

WALES

ENGLAND

✎ Read the sentences below and then tick the correct box. Are you surprised by any of your results?

	I knew that	I did not know that
The UK is four countries working together.		
England, Scotland, Northern Ireland and Wales have not always been united.		
Monarchs have ruled in these countries for hundreds of years.		
Monarchs used to be powerful, but now they are not.		
We have had a Parliament for hundreds of years.		
Parliaments used to be weaker than the monarch, but now they are more powerful.		

A UNITED KINGDOM?

The UK has changed from a kingdom in which battles and wars were often fought, to one where most people want to live together peacefully.

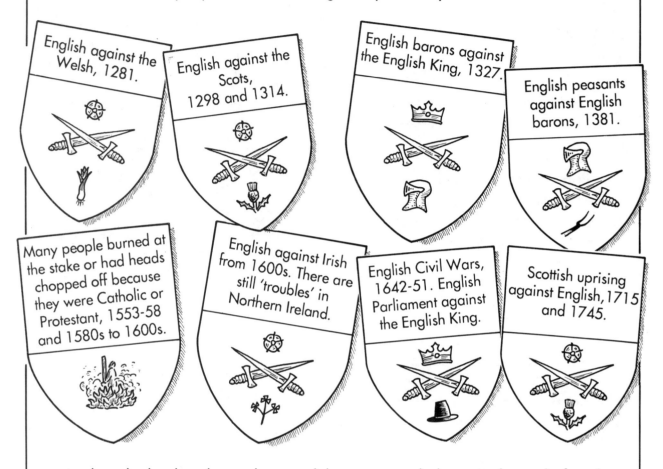

✎ Look at the battles above, then read the sentences below. At the end of each sentence write **Agree, Disagree** or **Need to know more.**

▲ The people who live in the British Isles have always got on well together. _____

▲ The Welsh accepted union with England hundreds of years ago. _____

▲ The Scots would not accept being ruled by the English. _____

▲ The Irish did not want union with England. _____

▲ The English got on very well with each other. _____

▲ Religious differences caused trouble in England. _____

▲ Ordinary English people were always happy with their rulers. _____

▲ The English King caused the Civil War in 1642. _____

TUDOR & STUART MONARCHS

✎ Read the fact box below.

● On each sash, fill in the monarch's name and the number of years they reigned. The first one is done for you.

── FACT BOX ──

Henry VII 1485-1509   Henry VIII 1509-1547   Edward VI 1547-1553
Mary I 1553-1558   Elizabeth I 1558-1603   James I 1603-1625
Charles I 1625-1649   Charles II 1660-1685   James II 1685-1688
William III and Mary II 1688-1702   Anne 1702-1714

POWER & PARLIAMENT 1500

Fact Box

- The first Parliament met in 1264.
- Parliaments met to agree to any new taxes the monarch needed.
- Dukes, earls, lords and bishops met in the House of Lords. They were rich and powerful and owned a lot of land.
- Important and rich 'Commoners' met in the House of Commons. They owned property, businesses or land.
- The common people did not own land or much property. They had no power.

✎ After reading this information decide who goes where on the diagram.
- Fill in the boxes with these words in the correct places:
  village labourers, monarch, dukes, beggars, craftsmen, rich businessmen, shopkeepers, women, bishops, merchants, town labourers, earls.
- Can you add any?

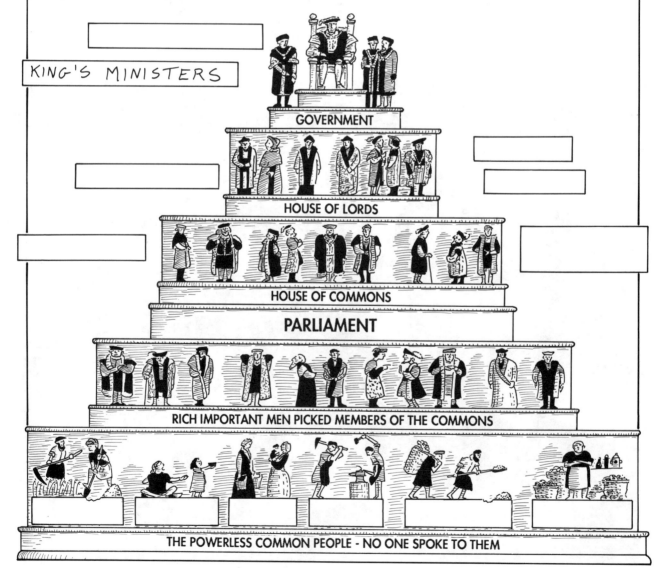

THE COMMON PEOPLE

Rich, powerful people often belong to titled families. They have titles such as duke, earl or lord. Anyone who does not belong to a titled family is a Commoner.

The first Parliaments had a House of Commons, but it was a House of rich Commoners.

Being a Commoner was not the same as being one of the common people. Most common people had to work in towns or the country for very low pay. Their lives were hard.

✎ Read the table below.
- ● Cross out the boxes you think are wrong.
- ● Outline in colour the boxes you think are correct.
- ● Has everyone agreed on all the answers? If you have given different answers, try to say why this has happened. Which is correct? Is anybody wrong?

The Common People

owned	big houses	lots of good farmland	some tools	lots of nice clothes	perhaps a pig or some chickens	a very small plot of land or 'garden'
worked as	craftsmen	lawyers	farm workers	soldiers	bishops	servants
lived in	towns	palaces	villages	small cottages	well-kept houses	unhealthy homes
ate and drank	best French wine	bread cheese milk	food from other countries	lots of fresh meat	peas and beans	cheap ale and wine sometimes
were able to	travel about the country easily	go to church	vote	rebel sometimes	go to good schools	take life easy
feared	illness	God	witches	having no work	being hungry	nothing
enjoyed	long, healthy lives	a good joke	long holidays	reading lots of books	listening to good storytellers	singing and dancing on feast days

HENRY RULES

Each of the sentences below has two endings.
- Read the sentences and underline the endings you agree with.

▲ I think that in 1509 — the Catholic Church did not want people to talk about new ways of believing in God.
— the Church liked new ideas about God.

▲ I think that Henry VIII — thought his own power was more important than religion.
— would respect the Pope too much to disagree with him.

▲ I think that in 1509 — many people believed in God but they thought there was a lot wrong with the Catholic Church.
— many people believed there was nothing wrong with the Church.

▲ I think that when Henry had a row with the Pope — most English people agreed with Henry.
— some English people felt very confused and upset.

KING, POPE AND PARLIAMENT

In 1527, Henry VIII wanted to divorce his Spanish, Catholic wife Catherine, because he wanted to marry Anne Boleyn.

✎ Use the strip cartoon to follow the story of Henry VIII and the Reformation Parliament. Put the words below each strip in the correct speech bubbles.

The Pope in Rome will not anger Catholic kings in Europe by agreeing to Henry's divorce.

Henry wants to divorce Catherine and marry Anne Boleyn.

Who says: *No, Henry, no divorce.*
Who says: *I'll ask the Pope for a divorce. Then I'll marry Anne and have a son.*

Many English people disagree with the divorce, so Henry needs powerful support.

Some powerful Englishmen hate the riches and power the Church has in England.

Who says: *I need strong supporters.*
Who says: *We don't like the Catholic Church's power.*

1529 – 1536

Parliament passes Henry's laws to end the power of the Catholic Church in England.

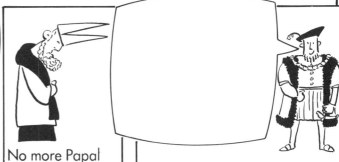

No more Papal power in England.

Henry alone rules.

Who says: *I'll use Parliament to break the power of the Catholic Church.*
Who says: *I'm Head of the Church of England. Englishmen must be loyal to me, not the Pope.*

PROTESTANTS AND POWER

Between 1500 and 1600 England changed from being a Catholic to a Protestant country. The Pope's power in England ended. Parliament wanted more power.

- Read each event below.

Heretics: people who speak against the Church. They are often burned at the stake.

1400s: Lollards, poor priests, speak out against the Catholic Church in England.

1517: in Germany, Martin Luther protests against the Catholic Church.

Protestant ideas spread.

1527: Henry VIII asks the Pope for a divorce from his Spanish, Catholic wife.

The Pope says "NO DIVORCE."

1529-36: English Parliament helps Henry VIII end the power of the Pope in England.

1547: Edward VI, the first Protestant king. Pictures and statues taken out of churches. Prayer book is now in English not Latin.

1553: Mary Tudor, a Catholic queen, tries to bring back the 'Old Religion'. Protestants are burned.

1558: Queen Elizabeth I, a Protestant, tries to bring peace but ...

... Catholics are said to be plotting against Elizabeth. Much chopping off of heads.

1580s: strict laws are passed against Catholics. It is not safe to be Catholic.

1600s: Puritan ideas spread. Puritans are very strict Protestants.

For many people being loyal to England means being a Protestant.

Some Puritans get rich. They are good at making lots of money.

Some Puritans become Members of Parliament.

Parliaments want more power.

A Protestant church in the 1600s

✎ Change happens for many reasons.
- If you think there is a strong link between two events, connect them with a chain.
- If you think there is a weak link, connect them with a thread.
  Some events may be linked more than once. Others may not have any links.

THE CIVIL WARS

In 1625 Charles I became the second Stuart King of England. Charles believed he ruled by Divine Right - God wanted him to be king.

Charles and his ministers disagreed with Parliament. The disagreements got so bad that on 23rd October 1642, a battle was fought at Edge Hill. The soldiers in both armies were Englishmen. The English Civil Wars had begun.

The Parliamentary army was led by the Earl of Essex, and the Royalist army was led by Prince Rupert, the King's nephew.

A Parliamentary Soldier   **A Royalist Soldier**

X First battle of the Civil War.

☐ Areas controlled by Parliament in 1643

▨ Areas controlled by Royalists in 1643

YORK

OXFORD
LONDON

BRISTOL

ENGLISHMEN WERE FIGHTING ENGLISHMEN.

✎ On the map:
- Write in the name of the first battle of the war.
- Shade in red the areas controlled by Parliament in 1643.
- Shade in blue the areas controlled by the Royalists in 1643.
- Mark in your city, town or village.
- Complete this sentence:

  I live in _____ . *In 1643 it was controlled by* _____ .

MONEY MATTERS

When Charles I came to the throne in 1625 he needed more money, so he asked for more taxes. The new taxes caused great arguments.

The King could not raise taxes without the agreement of Parliament.

✎ Read the speech bubbles and fill in the missing words.
Use the word box to help you.

SPECIALS! The Making of the UK: 1500 to 1750. F2934   © Folens.

RELIGION

Beautiful chapels were built for Queen Henrietta Maria, who was a French Catholic.

King Charles I was a Protestant and Governor of the Church of England. His wife, Henrietta Maria, was a Roman Catholic. Archbishop Laud, the leading Bishop of the Protestant Church of England, believed that beautiful churches made people feel more 'holy'. The changes he made in churches made people think that he was making England Roman Catholic again.

Puritans were very strict and their churches very plain. Many Puritans were put in prison and tortured for trying to spread their beliefs.

✎ Read the sentences in the chart below and draw a face which shows how people felt.

I am happy.

I am sad.

I don't care.

A Puritan church

Who is happy, sad, does not care:

	Most Protestants	Some members of the Church of England	Puritans	Catholics
about the way the King worships in Church?				
about the King's wife being a Catholic?				
about Archbishop Laud's changes in English churches?				
about Puritans being punished?				
about Catholics not being punished?				

MONARCH & PARLIAMENT 1625-1629

Follow the arguments between King Charles and Parliament.
✎ Choose from the lists of words and phrases the ones you think are correct.
Underline them.

1625-1628

Charles needed money to carry out his government plans.

⬇

His Parliaments wanted more say in government. They said 'NO' to his taxes.

SO ⬇

Charles I
A Got rid of his Parliaments.
B Set taxes anyway.
C Forced rich men to 'lend' him money.
D Put them in prison if they refused.

These events show Charles I was:
weak; strongminded; thoughtful; fair; determined; understanding; sure he was right; nervous; arrogant.

These events show Parliament was:
stronger than Charles;
strong enough to challenge Charles;
not as powerful as it wanted to be;
made up of brave men;
made up of men keen to govern;
right; wrong.

1628

Charles needed to have **more** money. He **had** to call a new Parliament.

➡

Parliament said that Charles could have more taxes if he agreed to the Petition of Right. (No taxes unless Parliament agreed and no one would go to prison without good reason.)

SO ⬇

Charles agreed to the Petition of Right, then dismissed Parliament in 1629 when it tried to put his **favourite**, the Duke of Buckingham, on trial. Charles ruled **without** Parliament for eleven years.

These events show Charles I was:
untrustworthy; sure he could and should rule without help from Parliament; sure he did not need help from England's rich classes; wise; foolish; right; wrong.

These events show Parliament was:
ready to get rid of monarchs; angry but loyal; ready to fight; not strong enough to stop Charles; wrong to want a say in government; right to want a say in government; wanted a say in government.

 SPECIALS! The Making of the UK: 1500 to 1750. F2934

DISMISSING PARLIAMENT

Use these two historical sources to answer the four questions on this sheet.

Source 1

A London poster about Charles and the Duke of Buckingham.

Who rules the Kingdom?
The King.
Who rules the King?
The Duke.
Who rules the Duke?
The Devil.
Let the Duke look to it.

Help: *'Let the Duke look to it'* means that the Duke should watch out! The Duke of Buckingham was the King's closest adviser (murdered 1628).

Source 2

Charles I got rid of Parliament in 1629. One MP held down the Speaker.

God's wounds! You shall sit 'til we please to rise.

Help: It was the Speaker's duty to do as the King said. *'God's wounds'* is an exclamation used at the time.

1. Read the two sources. Which one shows us that some Englishmen did not want to be ruled by a king?

2. What does the poster tell us of people's feelings about the Duke of Buckingham?

3. Do you think the MP shown in source 2 was for or against the King? Explain your answer.

4. Do you think the writer of the poster wanted to get rid of the King? Explain your answer.

PERSONAL RULE 1629-1640

The rows between the King and the dismissed Members of Parliament continued even though Charles was ruling without calling Parliaments.

✎ Read the events. Underline the words and phrases you think describe Charles best.

1629-1637

Charles ruled without Parliament. He set more taxes which the people did not like, such as the Ship Money tax.

⬇

Some men would not pay Ship Money. John Hampden and others said the tax was against the law. He tried to prove this in court.

BUT ⬇

England's judges said the King was not breaking the law.

These events show Charles I was:
sure he was ruling well;
knew only he had the right to govern;
arrogant;
not able to understand that times were changing;
not able to understand that rich people wanted a say in how they were taxed;
foolish;
wise.

1629-1637

Charles and Archbishop Laud did not like Puritans. Puritans were badly treated. Charles and Laud made the Church of England follow new rules. Some people said they were like Catholic rules.

➡

Charles wanted the strict Protestant Scots to use the English Prayer Book. They hated 'fussy' Church of England ways. The Scots said 'No' to the English Prayer Book. Charles said they must use it.

These events show Charles I was:
a good judge of events; not too good a judge of events; arrogant; fair; thoughtful; stubborn; wise; foolish; tolerant and ready to let people have their own beliefs; intolerant; ruling well.

SO ⬇

War with Scotland started. The English armies did not want to fight. The Scots beat the English. Charles could not pay his armies. By 1640 Charles was in trouble.

MONARCH & PARLIAMENT 1640-1641

By November 1640, the Scots had invaded England and Charles was in such trouble he had to call a Parliament he could not dismiss. The **Long Parliament** was here to stay - for twenty years!

Between 1640 and 1641 Parliament:
- punished the King's advisers. Thomas Wentworth, the Earl of Strafford, was executed. Archbishop Laud was put in prison.
- Parliament took control of all taxes and money matters.
- Parliament passed a law making the King call a new Parliament every three years. There could be no more personal rule.

What had changed?

✎ Tick only the boxes for which all three sentences are true.

Charles I	Parliament	Events	All three are true
The King was weak.	The King needed Parliament.	England had not been invaded.	
The King was strong.	Parliament was ready to take control.	England had been invaded.	
The King was in control but weak.	Parliament wanted to get rid of monarchs.	England had been invaded.	
The King was losing control.	Parliament was ready to take control but was still loyal to Charles.	England had been invaded.	

- Write a paragraph about Charles I. Use the following sentences to help you.
  I think Charles I was a _____ king. He acted _____ to others.
  He did make _____ mistakes. I think his worst mistake was _____ .

FOR OR AGAINST PARLIAMENT?

✎ Match the four labels to the pictures below:

| Puritans | Royalists | Common people | Merchant and wife |

● Read the comments around the pictures. Draw lines to link comments to the people you think would have made them. Some comments may link to more than one picture.

Kings of England have stolen the rights of freeborn Englishmen.

The Puritans go too far. Leading good lives does not mean leading dull ones.

The King and his friends live wicked, selfish lives. They will be punished.

The Church of England is not like a Protestant Church any more.

I do prefer a plainer church myself.

There is no harm in having beautiful churches and church services.

I can't see any sense in Englishmen fighting Englishmen.

Charles was wrong to tax us.

I don't know. If the Puritans have their way there'll be no fun for us village lads on Sundays.

Some of those Puritan preachers say good things. Some say people like us are as good as anyone else in England.

King or Parliament - our lives won't get any better.

I do not like the row between the King and Parliament, and do wish the King would give in ... But I will stand by him if it comes to war.

We are not very happy with what Charles is doing to the Church of England.

We are the ones who make England rich. Our MPs should control what the government spends.

FOR OR AGAINST THE KING?

In churches: people tore down altar rails and pictures. In London, crowds demonstrated against Charles.

In Ireland: Irish Catholics rebelled against English rule.

In Parliament: John Pym, Leader of the Commons, made a list of everything Charles had done badly. MPs were afraid Charles would use an army against them, instead of against the Irish rebels.

In the House of Commons: Charles tried to arrest Pym and four MPs. He took 300 soldiers with him but the five men were safe in the City of London. London was no longer a safe place for Charles, so he left.

Now there were two parties in England: Parliamentarians and Royalists ... it was WAR.

✎ Look at the four events above.
● In the box next to each sentence below, put the number of the event which shows the sentence is true.

▲ *Events in Ireland helped to bring about war in England.* ☐

▲ *People did not like the changes that had been made in churches.* ☐

▲ *The common people of London were not loyal to the King.* ☐

▲ *The five MPs knew that Charles wanted to arrest them.* ☐

▲ *Charles was a bad judge of what to do and when to do it.* ☐

▲ *Parliament could not trust the King with an army.* ☐

CIVIL WAR BATTLES

✎ Shade in red the parts of the country that were for Parliament (Parliamentarian).
Shade in blue the parts of the country that were for Charles (Royalist).

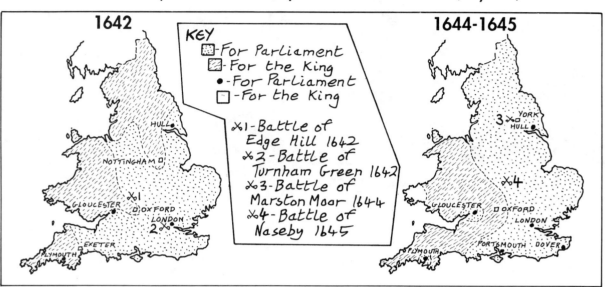

1642

1644-1645

KEY
- ▨ – For Parliament
- ▨ – For the King
- ● – For Parliament
- ☐ – For the King

✗1 – Battle of Edge Hill 1642
✗2 – Battle of Turnham Green 1642
✗3 – Battle of Marston Moor 1644
✗4 – Battle of Naseby 1645

✎ Some events have important results. Read the lists of events and results below.
Match up each event to its most likely result. Write correct letters in the boxes.

Events

▲ The Royalists only just won at Edge Hill, but they lost at Turnham Green. ☐

▲ Parliament controlled sea ports. ☐

▲ The Royalist cavalry (horse soldiers) was better than Parliament's. ☐

▲ The Royalist cavalry was not good at obeying orders. ☐

▲ Parliament had help in 1644 from the Scots, who had many good soldiers. ☐

▲ The soldiers Charles brought back from Ireland in 1644 were not a very strong force. ☐

Results

A The Royalists gained early control of battles easily.

B Parliament won at Marston Moor in the North of England.

C The King could not get help from other countries.

D The King did not capture London.

E They rode off to chase the enemy and left the foot soldiers.

F In 1645 Charles' army was soon beaten at the Battle of Naseby.

SPECIALS! The Making of the UK: 1500 to 1750. F2934 © Folens.

THE SOLDIERS

Parliament's men called the King's men **Cavaliers**. This was an insult because the word Cavalier was used to describe Spanish troops who were very cruel.

The King's men called Parliament's men **Roundheads**. This was also an insult. Royalists were making fun of the short hair worn by the young men of the London crowds. Some Puritan MPs also had short hair.

After 1644, Parliament's army was given a new nickname, **Ironsides**.

The men of the New Model Army were well trained and were paid. Many were strict Puritans. They were called Ironsides because they stood firm in battle.

'Buff coats' made of leather. They were lighter than armour but thick enough to give some protection.

Wooden cases for holding gunpowder.

A Roundhead

A Cavalier

✎ Follow the code below to colour the uniforms.

1 - blue or green	4 - russet (reddish-brown)	7 - grey (metal armour)
2 - white	5 - red	8 - dark brown
3 - yellow	6 - black	9 - light brown

NEWS AND HEADLINES

✎ Read the news reports and headlines below.
● Cut them out and match up the headlines to the correct reports.
● Underline in red the facts in each report.
● Underline in blue the writer's opinion in each report.

2nd July 1644
Today Royalist troops were beaten at Marston Moor, near York. Scottish troops fought for Parliament. "We fight on," said Prince Rupert, the King's nephew.

May 1645
"We are sick of war!" said Thomas Carter, 35, from Dorset. "When an army is near, the soldiers sleep in our houses and eat our food. They take our tools and horses. Well, it's got to STOP and we're the lads to stop it." He showed us the clubs and farm tools he and his mates will use to take on any army going into the area.

CRAZY COLONEL SIDES WITH TROOPS!

2nd July 1644
Amazing but true! A man working in the field at Marston Moor where the battle was about to start had to be told to clear off because the King and Parliament were at war. "What," he said, "Has them two fallen out then?"

14th June 1645
The New Model Army beat the Royalists at Naseby. Ironsides will not budge in battle. "God is on our side," they say. Is this the end of the road for Charles?

WAR AGAIN!

"IT'S GOD'S VICTORY," SAYS CROMWELL

DOWN BUT NOT OUT - SETBACK FOR KING

May 1647
Men in the New Model Army want their full back pay and ... wait for it ... THE VOTE! Some troublemakers, Levellers they call themselves, are saying all men should have the right to vote. Parliament is worried. Colonel Rainborough says the poorest men "have rights just like everyone else!" What next ... women voting?

WAR? WHAT WAR?

Summer 1648
Charles made a secret deal with the Scots in a bid to be a 'real' king again. It's war again, as Cromwell and Fairfax, in grim mood, march to put down the Royalists and Scots.

THOUSANDS OF MEN ARMED WITH CLUBS MARCH TO SHOW WHO'S BOSS

CHARLES MIGHT HAVE MADE HIS BIGGEST MISTAKE EVER!

WOMEN AND THE WAR

✎ Read the seven sources about women in the Civil War.
- Fill in the evidence sheet with what you think are the correct numbers.
- Talk about any different answers you have noticed in your groups.

SOURCE 1: From a letter from the wife of a Parliamentarian to her soldier son (1643):
My dear Ned ... I am full of sorrow. They say they will burn our barns. I am afraid they will place soldiers so near me there will be no way out ... Ask your father if it is best for me to leave Brampton, or by God's help to hold out ...

SOURCE 3: From a Parliamentary newspaper (1644) reporting that the home of Charlotte, Countess of Derby, had been taken. Lady Derby had helped defend the family home in the past. The paper spoke of her husband and said she was:
The better soldier of the two.

Women and the War - Evidence sheet

Conclusion reached	Evidence/source number.
Women were not afraid to fight.	
Women who supported the King were brave.	
Women who supported Parliament were brave.	
The war made women sad.	
Women acted as doctors.	
Women acted as fire-fighters.	
Women acted as soldiers.	
Women felt sorry for and helped enemy soldiers.	
Men thought women were brave.	

SOURCE 2: From a modern history book telling us how Lady Bankes and her daughters defended their home against Parliament's soldiers:
She and her daughters joined the soldiers on the castle walls in flinging stones and hot coals down on the attackers ... (1971)

SOURCE 4: Picture from a song sheet (1648) telling the story of a girl who was a drummer in the army until she had a baby. The song was called: *The Female Warrior.*

SOURCE 5: Lucy Hutchinson, wife of a Parliamentarian, looked after wounded soldiers and said she had:
... dressed all their wounds with good success ...
She helped Royalist soldiers too and said she:
... had done nothing but what she thought was her duty in humanity to them ... (1644)

SOURCE 6: From a school history book. It tells us about the women of Nottingham who kept watch in the town at night:
... for fires and to stop the Royalists from setting fire to any more ... (1966)

SOURCE 7: A woman called Doll Leake writing after hearing of another death:
... I cannot express (say) how unhappy I am ... (1649)

END OF WAR?

The first Civil War ended in 1646. The Royalists were beaten, but Parliament still had four main problems:

1 How could Parliament get Charles to do as it wanted?	**2** Parliament was afraid of the New Model Army. They disagreed about pay, religion and votes.
3 What could be done about the Irish Catholic rebels?	**4** The Scots wanted more influence in government.

✎ What did Charles think?
- Look carefully at the problems faced by Parliament, above.
- Fill in Charles' thought bubbles, choosing ideas from the list below.
  (*Note*: We do not know what Charles really thought. We can only guess from the way he acted.)

▲ *Too many people have died. I will stop fighting.*
▲ *Parliament and the army can't agree. I'll talk to both and get them fighting each other.*
▲ *If I agree to let the Scots have what they want, they'll fight for me.*
▲ *Perhaps Parliament is right. The monarch should do what it says.*
▲ *I am the King. These men have no right to hold me.*
▲ *I will not give up the fight.*
▲ *My loyal subjects will rise up and fight for me again.*

SPECIALS! The Making of the UK: 1500 to 1750. F2934 © Folens.

DEATH OF THE KING

Read the story board below about the death of Charles I.

1648 ①

The King made a deal with the Scots. War started again. ☐

②

The King was still Parliament's prisoner. Cromwell and the other army leaders called Charles a 'man of blood'. ☐

③

Most MPs did not want to put Charles on trial. Colonel Pride and his soldiers stopped MPs going into the House of Commons if they would not agree to the trial. ☐

④

Even Thomas Fairfax, who had led the New Model Army, would not agree to put the King on trial. When Fairfax's name was called from the list of judges his wife shouted out that ... ☐

November 1648 ⑤

During his trial, Charles would not take off his hat, showing he had no respect for those trying him. Many people agreed it was unlawful to try the King. But Cromwell said, "We'll cut off his head ... ☐

January 1649 ⑥

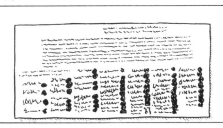

The order to execute the King was signed by 59 men. It is said that Cromwell held Richard Ingoldsby's hand down ... ☐

✎ Finish each caption by putting the words (**A - F**) in the correct place. Put the letter only in the correct box.

A he knew better than to judge the King.
B Only men agreeing with the army were allowed in.
C Parliament won again.
D with the crown on it."
E They wanted to punish Charles.
F to make him sign.

THE RISE OF CROMWELL

Read the events and fill in the scores for Cromwell (C) and Parliament (P).

Scores: +2 for more power   -1 for losing power   = for no change

1646. Parliament and the army argued over pay, power and religion.

1647. Cromwell kept the peace.

1648. War again. Some MPs wanted the New Model Army to lose, but Oliver's armies won again.

Score
C
P

1651. Cromwell beat the Irish and Royalist rebels, then the Scots and Royalist rebels.

Score
C
P

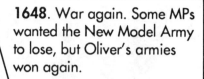

1649. Cromwell had the leaders of a mutiny in the army shot. No more Levellers in the army wanting a say.

1649. Only about 80 MPs left in the 'Rump' Parliament. Charles executed. No king, no Lords. England was a Commonwealth.

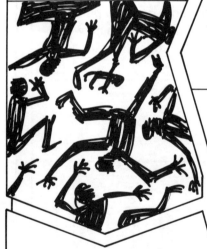

1653. Cromwell was made Lord Protector. He argued with Parliament.

Final
Score
C
P

1653. Cromwell said Parliament was not doing a good job. He took control. Good, 'Godly' men tried to rule, but failed.

Score
C
P

1655. Lord Protector, Cromwell, and his Major Generals ruled England without Parliament for nearly two years. There were some rebellions against Cromwell's rule.

OPINION POLL

✎ Fill in the two opinion poll sheets below.
- ● Fill in the first one as if you are an ex-soldier who fought with the New Model Army.
- ● Fill in the second one as if you are an ex-Royalist soldier.

Ex-New Model Army

	Strongly agree	Do not know	Strongly disagree
Cromwell should try harder to get on with Parliament.			
Cromwell should go on ruling with the help of his Generals.			
All men should vote for Members of Parliament.			
Cromwell should not agree to be king.			
Cromwell should not be king because he is a Commoner.			
Cromwell should not be king because we should not have kings.			
Cromwell should be called 'His Highness' even if he is not king.			
Crowmell should be able to choose who rules when he dies.			
We should bring back the House of Lords.			
We should bring back the Stuart kings.			

Ex-Cavalier

	Strongly agree	Do not know	Strongly disagree
Cromwell should try harder to get on with Parliament.			
Cromwell should go on ruling with the help of his Generals.			
All men should vote for Members of Parliament.			
Cromwell should not agree to be king.			
Cromwell should not be king because he is a Commoner.			
Cromwell should not be king because we should not have kings.			
Cromwell should be called 'His Highness' even if he is not king.			
Crowmell should be able to choose who rules when he dies.			
We should bring back the House of Lords.			
We should bring back the Stuart kings.			

Oliver Cromwell died in 1658. His son did not want to rule and in 1659 one of Cromwell's Major Generals, General Monck, took control. He allowed Royalist MPs back into Parliament.

In 1660 Charles I's eldest son came back to rule England, as Charles II.

Who was glad? 😊   Who was sad? 😢

Ex- _____   Ex- _____

THE SPEAKER & PARLIAMENT

✎ The Speaker is an important person in Parliament. He or she is responsible for keeping the MPs in order, and allowing them each to have their say.

● Read each sentence in the diagram below.

● Shade the seven correct sentences and you will find the Speaker's hat.

The House of Commons in 1651

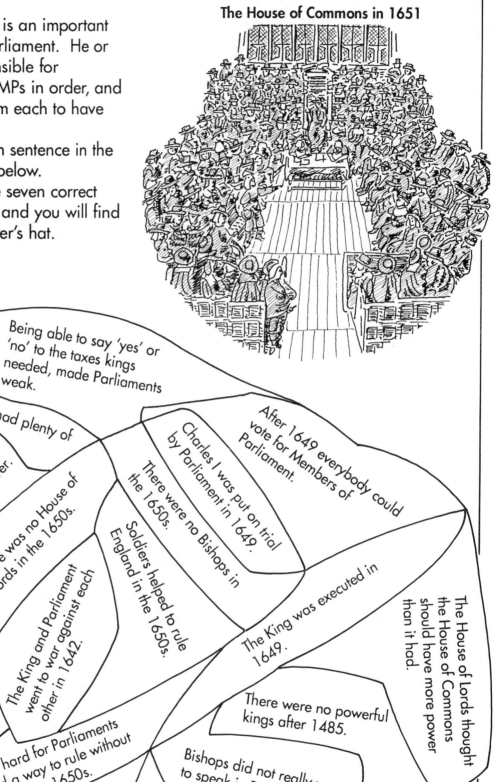

Being able to say 'yes' or 'no' to the taxes kings needed, made Parliaments weak.

Kings always had plenty of money.

Parliaments were happy to let kings have all the power.

After 1649 everybody could vote for Members of Parliament.

Charles I was put on trial by Parliament in 1649.

There were no Bishops in the 1650s.

There was no House of Lords in the 1650s.

Soldiers helped to rule England in the 1650s.

The King and Parliament went to war against each other in 1642.

The King was executed in 1649.

The House of Lords thought the House of Commons should have more power than it had.

Parliaments always cared about the common people.

There were no Parliaments after 1485.

It was hard for Parliaments to find a way to rule without a king in the 1650s.

There were no powerful kings after 1485.

Bishops did not really want to speak in Parliament.

Parliaments always agreed the taxes kings needed were fair.

Kings and Parliaments always agreed with each other after 1485.

SPECIALS! The Making of the UK: 1500 to 1750. F2934

RESTORATION

In the 1660s, Samuel Pepys kept a diary. He wrote about his life and what was happening in England at the time.

✎ If the people in the pictures had kept diaries, which of the events below do you think would have pleased or worried them? Write the correct numbers on the pages of their diaries. The first one has been done for you.

We were worried by	We were pleased about
	1

Rich lord and lady of the King's court

We were worried about	We were happy about
	1

Rich merchant and his wife

We were upset by	We were happy with
1	

Dissenters

We were happy about	We were worried about
1	
We didn't care about	

Common people

1. Theatres re-opened, sports and village games were allowed again.
2. Music was allowed in Church again.
3. Strict laws were passed against Puritans and Dissenters (Protestants who would not join the Church of England).
4. 1665: plague broke out in London and many people died.
5. 1666: the Great Fire of London burned for four days.
6. 1673: laws were passed stopping Catholics from holding important jobs.
7. Scientists were given support by Charles.
8. John Bunyan's book A Pilgrim's Progress was a best-seller. He was a Puritan put in prison for preaching his ideas. He had fought for Parliament.
9. 1678: the Popish Plot. People were afraid there would be another civil war.
10. 1670s: Parliament split into two parties. Tories supported Charles and his brother; Whigs tried to stop Catholic James from being the next king.
11. All sorts of artists, writers and craftsmen did well.

THE WHEEL OF HISTORY

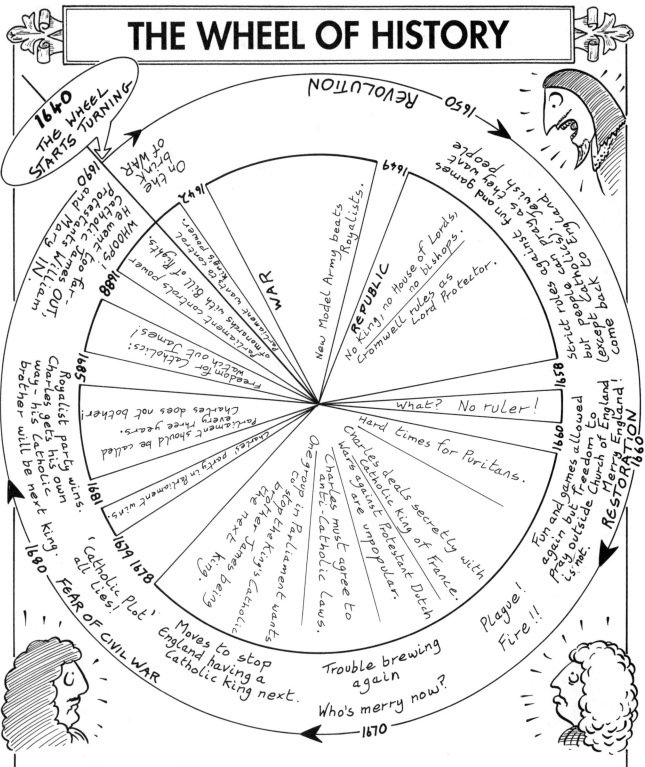

1640 THE WHEEL STARTS TURNING

1650 REVOLUTION

On the brink of WAR

1690 Catholic James and Protestant Mary IN. WHOOPS! He went too far — William IN, James OUT.

1642 WAR

1688 Parliament controls power with Bill of Rights.

Parliament wants to control monarch's power.

1649 REPUBLIC New Model Army beats Royalists.

No King, no House of Lords, no bishops. Cromwell rules as Lord Protector.

1685 Freedom for Catholics! Watch out James!

1681 Parliament should be called every three years. Charles does not bother!

Royalist party wins. Charles gets his own way — his Catholic brother will be next King.

1679 1678 Charles's party in Parliament wins.

One group in Parliament wants to stop the King's brother James being the next King.

Moves to stop England having a Catholic king next.

Charles must agree to anti-Catholic laws.

Charles deals secretly with Catholic king of France. Wars against Protestant Dutch are unpopular.

Hard times for Puritans.

What? No ruler!

1660 1658

Fun and games allowed again but freedom to pray outside Church of England is not.

Strict rules against fun and games as they want people to finish (?) go against England to live Catholic to (except back) come

RESTORATION 1660 Merry England!

Plague! Fire!!

Trouble brewing again

Who's merry now?

1670

1680 FEAR OF CIVIL WAR

'Catholic Plot' all lies!

✎ Turn the wheel to follow the story.
● Read the events in the list below.

1. 1642 - Civil War
2. 1649 - Death of Charles I
3. 1658 - Death of Cromwell
4. 1660 - Charles II is the King

5. 1678-79 - Plots and panic
6. 1681 - No Parliaments
7. 1685 - Catholic James II is the King
8. 1688 - The Glorious Revolution

● Fill in the events on the eight blank spokes.

FOLLOW THE CROWN

Follow the crown to see how the bloodless, Glorious Revolution of 1688 ended the line of Stuart monarchs and passed the crown to the German Hanovers.

● Draw a crown in the space above each king and queen. James I is already crowned.
● Draw a paper crown on the heads of the Stuarts who thought they should rule. In England the crown usually passes to the eldest son.

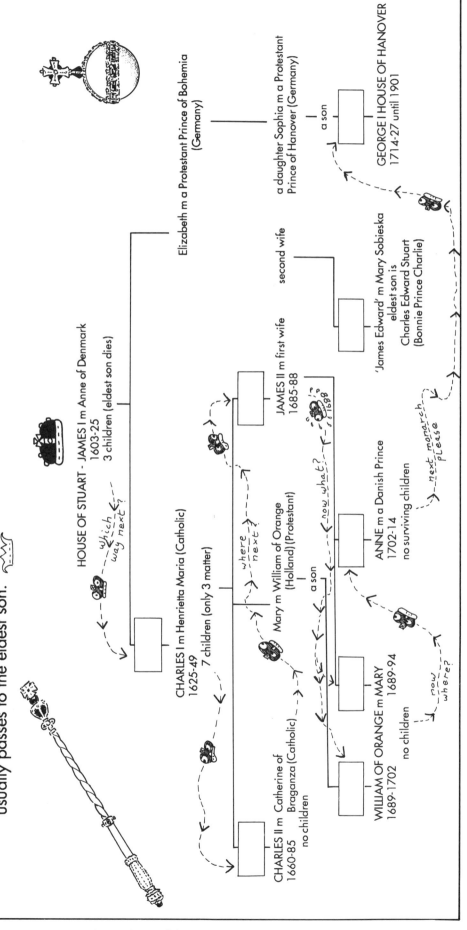

HOUSE OF STUART - JAMES I m Anne of Denmark
1603-25
3 children (eldest son dies)

which way next?

CHARLES I m Henrietta Maria (Catholic)
1625-49
7 children (only 3 matter)

where next?

Elizabeth m a Protestant Prince of Bohemia (Germany)

CHARLES II m Catherine of Braganza (Catholic)
1660-85
no children

Mary m William of Orange (Holland) (Protestant)

a son

JAMES II m first wife
1685-88

second wife

ANNE m a Danish Prince
1702-14
no surviving children

now what?

1688

'James Edward' m Mary Sobieska
eldest son is
Charles Edward Stuart
(Bonnie Prince Charlie)

WILLIAM OF ORANGE m MARY
1689-1702   1689-94
no children

now where?

next monarch please

a daughter Sophia m a Protestant Prince of Hanover (Germany)

a son

GEORGE I HOUSE OF HANOVER
1714-27 until 1901

JOINT MONARCHS

✎ Here are William and Mary wrapped up in the Bill of Rights in 1688.

THE BILL OF RIGHTS

No monarch can be Catholic or marry a Catholic. The best jobs and education, the right to vote or be an MP are for members of the Church of England only.

Monarchs must take notice of laws passed by Parliament. Parliaments must be elected every three years.

Monarchs are to be given money by Parliaments to pay for their everyday costs.

Monarchs still command the army, but Parliaments help to control it and keep it disciplined.

✎ Read these sentences. Fill in the boxes at the end of each sentence with **Cannot do that** or **Can do that**.

	Cannot do that	Can do that
After 1688 what happens if:		
▲ the monarch's son wants to marry a Catholic		
▲ Parliament passes a law the monarch does not like and he/she wants to change it		
▲ the Leader of the House of Commons wants to command the army		
▲ an MP says the monarch should pay his/her own bills		
▲ a Catholic wants to be an MP		
▲ a Parliament wants to stay in power for four years?		

● Read the following sentence and write why you agree or disagree with it:

After 1688, the monarch had more power than Tudor and early Stuart monarchs.

I agree because _____

or

I disagree because _____

SPECIALS! The Making of the UK: 1500 to 1750. F2934   © Folens.

ROAD SIGNS

Read the directions below, and write them on the correct sign posts.

▲ To the future
▲ To the past
▲ To Catholic England
▲ To the English Republic
▲ To the Modern Age
▲ To the United Kingdom

PLOTS AND PRAYERS

After the 1530s, more and more English people became Protestant.

✎ Read each event below.
- Did it make people support or turn against Catholics? Shade the correct arrow for each event.
- Put a big **!** against the events which show how Catholics were trapped by Protestants in power.

1560s to 1580s
Catholics plot against Elizabeth I. They want Catholic Mary Queen of Scots to be queen. Elizabeth's chief minister knows about the plots but lets the plotters carry on. Mary is executed in 1587.

OPINIONS

Against Catholics   For Catholics

1605
The Gunpowder Plot. Catholics plot to blow up Protestant King James I and Parliament, and to take over the government with Spanish help. Today, many people think the Gunpowder Plot was a government plot to make English people more anti-Catholic.

OPINIONS

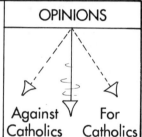

Against Catholics   For Catholics

1678-79
The Popish Plot. Titus Oates, a Protestant, says he knows of a plot by Catholics to kill Charles II. The King does not believe it but nine Catholics are executed and thousands flee from London. Titus Oates made up the whole plot!

OPINIONS

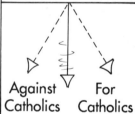

Against Catholics   For Catholics

1685
Monmouth's Uprising. The Protestant Duke of Monmouth, a son of Charles II, leads Protestant rebels against his Catholic uncle, James II. About 6 000 common people join him. They are beaten. Monmouth begs for his life. He and 200 followers are executed.

OPINIONS

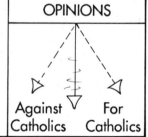

Against Catholics   For Catholics

1715 and 1745
The Jacobite Rebellions. The Catholic son of James II calls himself James III. He leads Scottish Highland Chiefs against England in 1715. They are beaten. In 1745, his son, Charles Edward Stuart, 'Bonnie Prince Charlie' tries again and is beaten at Culloden.

OPINIONS

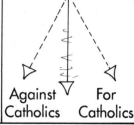

Against Catholics   For Catholics

RELIGION, POLITICS AND SCIENCE

✎ When an old idea falls, new ones take its place.
● Write the new ideas in the correct order on top of the old 'fallen' idea.

Religious ideas

People should be free to write, preach and spread ideas.

People do not need priests or bishops.

People should be free to pray as they want.

3.

2.

1.

Churches and priests should tell people how to think about God.

Blown down by Puritan thinking.

Political ideas

The King's right to rule is based on the promise to rule well.

Monarchs have no power.

Parliaments have a right to get rid of a king who rules badly.

3.

2.

1.

Monarchs rule by Divine Right.

Blown down by Parliament's challenge to Charles I.

Social ideas

There is nothing in the Bible to say some are rich, some poor.

All people are equal.

Poor people have rights. They should vote.

3.

2.

1.

God made people rich or poor.

Blown down by Levellers and Diggers who have read the Bible carefully.

Scientific ideas

What we know must be based on real events.

Scientists can ask about anything and test their ideas.

Ideas proved by science to be true are best.

3.

2.

1.

Ideas based on fear and superstition.

Blown down by 17th century science.

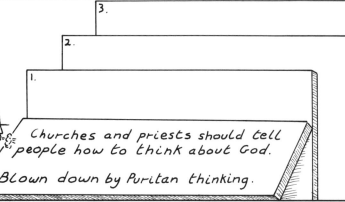

SCIENCE

In the 17th century, science paved a new path.

✎ Write the names of the scientists on the correct new paving stones.

Francis Bacon (early1600s)
Knowledge must come from experiment and proof.

John Napier (1614)
Invents logarithms.

William Harvey (1628)
Shows how blood moves round the body.

Royal Society (1660)
Scientists and thinkers meet to talk about new ideas.

Robert Boyle (1662)
Studies chemicals and gases.

Isaac Newton (1660s-1700s)
Studies light, gravity, movement and mathematics.

Robert Hooke (1665)
Invents new microscope.

Edmund Halley (1682)
Studies paths of comets.

Halley invents diving bell. **(1690)**

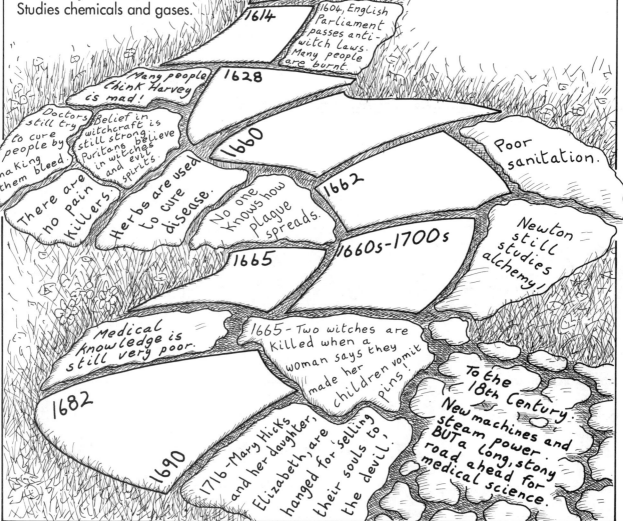

UNITING THE KINGDOM

✎ Use the number code to colour all the flags:　1 = red　3 = blue
2 = white　4 = green

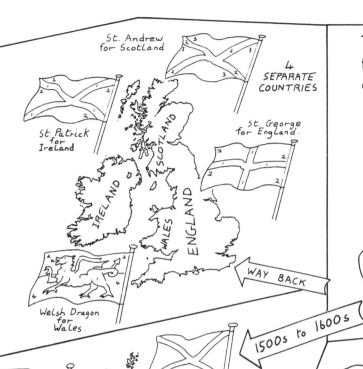

The English takeover began in the 1100s. The Scots, Irish and Welsh fought back, but …

● Finish the sentence:

The flag which has not been used to build up the Union Flag is the flag of _____ .

IRELAND

After the late 1550s, England was a Protestant country but Ireland was still Roman Catholic. The English grip on Ireland became tighter over the years.

In 1640 Irish Catholics owned fifty-nine per cent of Irish land. Protestant settlers from England and Scotland owned the rest. In 1658 Irish Catholics owned twenty-two per cent of Irish land. By 1714 Irish Catholics owned only seven per cent of Irish land.

✎ Shade in green the section of each pie chart that shows Irish Catholic land ownership.

1640

Land owned by Irish Catholics.

1658

Land owned by Irish Catholics.

1714

Irish Catholic Land.

✎ Read the events below.
● Write the event letter in the correct box on the diagram to show why Irish Catholics lost their land.

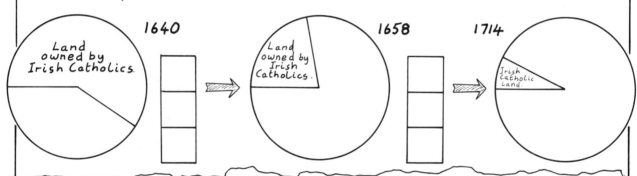

a) 1641: rebellion against the English in Ireland. Protestants were killed.

b) 1649-50: Cromwell ended the Irish rebellion. He used great cruelty against Catholics.

c) More land was given to Protestant settlers.

d 1688: Catholic James II was removed. In 1689 he invaded Ireland with French troops. He wanted to attack England from Ireland to get back his throne.

e) 1690: William III's troops beat James' troops at the Battle of the Boyne. Catholics were treated cruelly again.

f) More Irish Catholic land was given to Protestant settlers.

● Finish the sentence:
The English were always afraid Ireland could be used _____

_____

STUART TO HANOVER

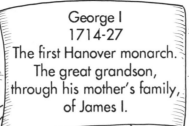

George I
1714-27
The first Hanover monarch.
The great grandson,
through his mother's family,
of James I.

Charles Edward Stuart
He was known as the
'Young Pretender' and
'Bonnie Prince Charlie'.

James Edward
The 'Old Pretender'.
The son of James II and
his second wife.

Queen Anne
1702-14
The last Stuart monarch.
She was the second
daughter of James II and
left no living child.

George II
1727-60

George III
1760-1820

George IV
1820-30

✎ Read the sentences below.

▲ After Parliament passed the Bill of Rights in 1689, no English monarch could be Catholic
or marry a Catholic.

▲ In Tudor times Parliament could never have passed a law controlling a monarch.

▲ In 1701 Parliament passed a law to make sure the crown was passed on to the Protestant
Hanovers and not the Queen's Catholic half-brother, James.

▲ In Tudor times the crown passed to the next brother or sister in line. Parliament could not
say who would be the next monarch.

▲ After 1688 the monarch had to call a Parliament every three years. He or she could not
rule without Parliament.

▲ In Tudor times the monarch called Parliament if and when he or she wanted.

▲ In the 1700s the monarch still picked the men who would run the government.

▲ In the 1500s the monarch picked the men who ran the government.

▲ In the 1700s Parliament controlled the money the monarch needed.

▲ In the 1500s the monarch needed Parliament to agree to taxes.

● For each sentence that shows the monarch to be powerful, draw a crown on
the correct scale. ♛

● For each sentence that shows Parliament to be powerful, draw a scroll on
the correct scale. 📜

Monarch   Parliament   Monarch   Parliament

1500s   1700s

● Finish the sentence: *By the 1700s the power to rule had shifted to* _____ .

PARLIAMENT AND PRIME MINISTERS

In the 18th century the monarch's government ministers had to be backed by Parliament.

George I became king in 1714. He spoke little English and he spent a lot of time back home in Hanover. He left the job of running government meetings to Robert Walpole, his chief minister.

Robert Walpole

There were two parties in Parliament, the **Tories** and **Whigs**. The Whigs strongly backed the Protestant Hanover kings, while some Tories backed the Stuart, King James III of Scotland. The Whigs controlled English government for many years after George I became king. Many Whigs were very rich landowners.

Democracy means rule by the people; people at least have the right to vote.
● Read the democracy checklist below.
● Tick the boxes to show whether 18th century England was democratic.
● Use your answers to work out who really ruled in 18th century England.

Democracy	*18th century England - democratic?*	Yes	No
Every adult woman can vote.	*No women voted.*		
Every adult man can vote.	*Only rich men voted.*		
Women can be MPs.	*Only men could be MPs.*		
An MP's religion does not matter.	*Only members of the Church of England could be MPs.*		
A person's religion does not affect the right to vote.	*Catholics could not vote.*		
MPs must not pay voters for their support.	*Voters were paid to vote for one man or the other.*		
No one can be forced to vote one way or the other.	*Powerful men 'leaned' on voters to vote the 'right' way.*		
Voting is done in secret.	*Voters said which man they supported in a public meeting.*		

Who voted? _____

Who ruled? _____

CLASSES

✏ Look at the pictures on this page and read the list of words in the word box.

well-fed	powerful
overworked	educated
powerless	well clothed
ignorant	badly housed
very rich	rich
hungry	desperate
landless	homeless
content	landowning

- Choose words from the box which describe the different classes of people. Write them next to the pictures. Some words may describe more than one class of people.
- Add some words of your own.

Upper Class

_____

_____

_____

_____

Middle Class

_____

_____

_____

_____

Lower Class

_____

_____

_____

_____

squires
merchants
bankers
aristocrats
Clergy
poorer gentry
Well-off common people
clerks
doctors
Schoolmasters
millers
Handloom weavers
skilled craftsmen
small Farmers
village craftsmen
InnKeepers
Unskilled workers
servants
soldiers
milkmaids
rioters
country Labourers
beggars
Criminals
town Labourers

THE RACE

✏️ Follow the race from 1509 to the 20th century.
● Fill in the missing names.

SPECIALS! The Making of the UK: 1500 to 1750. F2934 © Folens.

PUPIL RECORD SHEET

Name: _____   Class: _____

Activity Sheet	Completed	Understood	Nearly understood	Not understood
Did You Know?				
A United Kingdom?				
Tudor and Stuart Monarchs				
Power and Parliament 1500				
The Common People				
Henry Rules				
King, Pope and Parliament				
Protestants and Power				
The Civil War				
Money Matters				
Religion				
Monarch and Parliament 1625-29				
Dismissing Parliament				
Personal Rule 1629-38				
Monarch and Parliament 1640-41				
For or Against Parliament?				
For or Against the King?				
Civil War Battles				
The Soldiers				
News and Headlines				
End of War?				
Women and the War				
Death of the King				
The Rise of Cromwell				
Opinion Poll				
The Speaker and Parliament				
Restoration				
The Wheel of History				
Follow the Crown				
Joint Monarchs				
Road Signs				
Plots and Prayers				
Religion, Politics and Science				
Science				
Uniting the Kingdom				
Ireland				
Stuart to Hanover				
Parliament and Prime Ministers				
Classes				
The Race				

TEACHER RECORD SHEET

Name: _____   Class: _____

Activity Sheet	Completed	Understood	Not understood	Action
Did You Know?				
A United Kingdom?				
Tudor and Stuart Monarchs				
Power and Parliament 1500				
The Common People				
Henry Rules				
King, Pope and Parliament				
Protestants and Power				
The Civil War				
Money Matters				
Religion				
Monarch and Parliament 1625-29				
Dismissing Parliament				
Personal Rule 1629-38				
Monarch and Parliament 1640-41				
For or Against Parliament?				
For or Against the King?				
Civil War Battles				
The Soldiers				
News and Headlines				
End of War?				
Women and the War				
Death of the King				
The Rise of Cromwell				
Opinion Poll				
The Speaker and Parliament				
Restoration				
The Wheel of History				
Follow the Crown				
Joint Monarchs				
Road Signs				
Plots and Prayers				
Religion, Politics and Science				
Science				
Uniting the Kingdom				
Ireland				
Stuart to Hanover				
Parliament and Prime Ministers				
Classes				
The Race				

 SPECIALS! The Making of the UK: 1500 to 1750. F2934